TRACES OF
PILGRIMAGE

 FriesenPress

One Printers Way
Altona, MB R0G 0B0
Canada

www.friesenpress.com

Consuelo España - Spanish translation of "Heart"

ISBN
978-1-03-830932-7 (Hardcover)
978-1-03-830931-0 (Paperback)
978-1-03-830933-4 (eBook)

POETRY, SUBJECTS & THEMES, NATURE

Distributed to the trade by The Ingram Book Company

Traces of Pilgrimage

Poems

Tom McKoy

for Vivienne and Thomas,
something solid

"Enjoy every sandwich."
—Warren Zevon

TABLE OF CONTENTS

1

The Light of Life

WE GO BACK

The comfort of talk
with an old friend—
a thumb rubbed
on well-worn
sea glass.
Because your memory
is more lucid
than mine,
I look to you
to remember
who I am,
make it worthy
of celebration.

DANCE STEPS

My friend Steve is a beautiful dancer.
He moves with grace
leading each partner
around the floor
with a steady hand,
keeping time to whatever
tune is in the air.

When I was young
as a break from all-boy school
I went to dancing class:
first Tuesday afternoons,
then Friday nights, and finally
Saturday evenings. I never learned
the steps, never learned to lead,
but relished embracing those girls,
body to body, in a sanctioned manner.

Now, even though I get dizzy
easily and have no sense
of rhythm, I love to dance;
to hold a woman close,
to move together to music.
My wife is an effortless dancer.
Sometimes when we
dance together she will ask,
What are
you doing?

TOM MCKOY

BEACH BOND WITH ELLEN

In memory
sunsets tend to bleed
into each other

except once
and only once
years ago

both of us sure
only because the other
had seen it also

we stood side by side
above Lighthouse Beach
and saw the green flash—

just as the great ball blinked itself
into the unclouded ocean

an instant of brilliant bloom.

El Corazón

un músculo de recintos por el que corre la sangre
es un pedazo de carne trabajador
el corazón de mi padre dejó de latir en 2004
el corazón de mi hermano dejó de latir en 1967
el mío late todavía y los abraza
en realidad no es el corazón sino la mente
el lugar en el que la mente se reúne con el corazón
fisuras de la mente que se cruzan con los recintos del corazón
a veces hay personas que estan en mi corazón sin merecerlo
y aunque no ya estén en el sus recintos están repletos
los vivos y los muertos se toman las manos
a veces mi mente vaga por su propio camino
pero mi corazón está conmigo
íntegro durante el trayecto completo

Spanish translation by Consuelo España

Tom McKoy

Heart

a chambered muscle that pumps blood
a hard-working hunk of flesh
my father's heart stopped in 2004
my brother's in 1967
mine still beats and encompasses them
it's not really the heart that we speak of, rather it's the mind
or that junction where the mind and heart connect
fissures of the mind intersecting chambers of the heart
sometimes people who don't belong enter my heart
after they leave it is still a crowded room
the living and the dead all holding hands
sometimes my mind wanders its own way
but my heart stays with me
the whole journey

Small Comfort

I have friends in whom
the light of life is fading.

When I see
their loved ones
out in the world

I always ask
what that is
like.

Out of kindness
they reply.

In their eyes
I read
the burden of care.

The small talk never
cures the unwell
or diminishes the weight.

Afterwards
they don't need
my hug—
but I want theirs.

Ashes

"I'm gonna cover myself with the ashes of youth."
—Nathaniel Rateliff

I
During gatherings
with old schoolmates
we sometimes stir
the embers of nostalgia.
If they burst into flame
I back away.

II
I had a lover once
who had a prosthetic leg.
She had been hit
by a drunk Australian
State Policeman
driving 100 miles an hour.

I had a lover once who
took me to a beach at night
to wade into waves
of bioluminescence. She
wanted to marry; I did not.
She moved to a sheep farm
in New Zealand and married a Kiwi.

I had a lover once
who lost twins
through miscarriage,
then adopted a child
from a mother in Mexico
who could not cope
with yet another offspring.

III
My adolescent self never
told my younger brother
that I loved him.
Sorrow nudges me
from his tombstone.

Elements of a Father's Day

The sound of a baseball game
announced on the radio,
a green 1950 Plymouth station wagon,
a pack of Lucky Strikes,
a cracked and faded black-and-white photograph
of a still-young smiling World War II Marine pilot
on one knee, his arm around a boy
who has one hand up
to shade his eyes from the sun.

Or perhaps the boy is trying
to shield himself from
the heartache already radiating
from the pilot's destiny;
a life in which each day
will be lived as though
going off to war the next:
one more drink,
one more girl,
one more hand of Gin Rummy.

In the end it is the ebullient charm
that is remembered
by friends, ex-wives, and children,
sharing laughter at stories
of bad-boy adventures
and long-ago trysts
that once damaged
most of our hearts.
Each, *I'll be home for dinner,*
each, *I will see you Sunday,*
fades as forgiveness is granted
by those most let down.

The litter of sorrow scatters
as it blows across
the flat government-issued stone,
carved with name, rank,
and two dates.

MEMORY'S KISS

Playing tag on a tiny
square of lawn
my two little boys and I
their white-blond hair
flying
arms extended, wild giggles,
hearts pounding.

The boys are now grown
and tattooed
with beards
going gray.

The lawn may be
the site of
some new owner's
hot tub.

Still, for me,
the three of us
tumble gleefully
forever.

JOG INTO THE NIGHT

After a day of rain, during a jog into twilight,
the neighborhood street is alive completely.

Vintage roses, a large magnolia, a redwood tree,
even the lowly oxalis, all radiate an inner light.

      My father is everywhere

Tall trees bow low, shedding droplets
in small staccato splats. Unseen frogs blurp with pleasure.

Two doves fly up from the curb, sounding a curious combination
of excited wing flaps and soft-throated coos.

      My father is everywhere still

Jogging down the street into the coming night,
my shoes slap-slapping on wet concrete,

I am here, knowing the moment, and yet,
and yet,

      Certainly, my father is dust

still I keep on
running.

You Must Remember

A song on the radio:
"The Glory of Love"
recorded in 1936
by Benny Goodman.
My father was 12,
my mother, 10.
Would their parents
have danced to it?
Are they dancing together now?
All of them, even my mother,
who is still alive. In her sleep
does she dance with my father?
So handsome, charming,
a smile to dazzle the sky
the perfume of other women
momentarily washed away.

Reaching for Sleep

When I was six and could not fall asleep
my mother would sit by the bed,
stroke my forehead, and sing,
Frère Jaques, Frère Jaques,
Dormez vous? Dormez vous?
Sonnez les matines, Sonnez les matines.
ding ding dong, ding ding dong.

Fifty years later, I wake at night often
drenched in sweat, some anxiety
getting its kicks at the expense
of my solid snooze. Each time I come close
to dropping off, a new twist enters
my head and I roll over
to deal with a revised distress.

After an hour or two, I am able
to depart this anxious plane
envisioning Cascade Head on the Oregon Coast,
where wildflowers and prairie grasses wave
five hundred feet above the surf line,
and peregrine falcons soar against
billows of cumulus clouds.

Then at last,
those blessed bells
ding ding dong.

Tom McKoy

Dementia Scramble

in Memory of Mary Tilghman, 1927–2021

Sitting side by side we open the cracked leather photo album.
There you are with your third husband at the golf club. Next
to it you are in Pittsburgh at a party with your first husband;
all skinny ties and women smoking. Next to that, your
grandchildren, five young men together in the backyard at
Martha's Vineyard. Then a blank page. After that you are an
18-year-old debutante, and there is that story about being
robbed at gunpoint in the lobby of the Barclay Hotel. A pause
at the photo of your middle child, killed in a car accident in
1967, his shy smile while holding an enormous fish. You say
again how you will never get over the loss. Then your daughter,
her three sons and her in-laws at the beach. You remember
her father-in-law, Tony, how happy he was just to sit in the
sun on the dock and read. Then a blank section, followed by
Christmas cards with photos of families whose names you
cannot recall. *Happy Holidays.* Two empty pages. A black and
white, your dad fishing. Blank page. End of album.

BIRTHRIGHT

My father's sins
traverse through time
from his father's sins
inescapable line
through me
to my sons
whose father's sins
are mine.

BITTER TEA

when we argue I slap my love
with silence

neither of us understands
what gives

like a well-intentioned
but failed utopia

brown grass overgrows
our celebratory gathering place

the earth has warped
so the front door scrapes

where only yesterday
it swung freely

after time and tears and talk
the weeds are cleared

the door swings again but
for a small eternity

our tea will taste
of salt

Dream Work

The ex-wife used to tell me
her dreams.

I was never interested;
they just didn't make sense.

Last night I dreamed
about a bumper sticker.

It read—
Marriage is like making sausage.

I spent a long time
trying to figure out what it meant

but that was a dream
as well.

Four Falls

1.
three years old
out the second-story window
down past the kitchen window
where my mother was watching
landed in the cellar window-well
full of leaves
not a scratch

2.
after smoking some dope
I made love
with my good friend's gal
passion spent we both smiled
the bruise of remorse not yet
tender to the touch

3.
jogging out to the lighthouse
I watch the full moon
rise over Pleasure Point
catch my toe
go down hard

4.
looking at the calendar
spring is in the air
yet each day I wake
to a layer of frost
on my bones

BIRTHDAY PRESENCE (FOR ELLEN)

The years are as wind
absent substance
absent form.

I orient myself
in time
and space
by the nearness
of you.

This is your gift to me:
a specific habitation,
a touch, an embrace—
the only tangible
under the vast
unknowable sky.

II

If We Wander Too Far

Alpha Female, Wapiti Lake Wolf Pack

Yellowstone National Park

I am called Daughter of White Lady.
Hooked up last year
with that big wandering male 755M.
He got me good. Today our pack has
five pups here in Hayden Valley.

Long winter in the den.
Damn, did my teats hurt.
Then months of puking up
meat for them to gnaw. Now,
thanks to gods of blood and marrow,
the litter hunts with the pack.

Not long ago our kind almost vanished:
hunted, trapped, poisoned. These days
the pack prospers; except
if we wander too far,
go for beef or lamb,
it ends badly.

In the morning, when the fog lifts,
all those ghost creatures in RVs
will be waiting, watching
to catch a glimpse of any one of us.
Think I'll go outside, have a pee—
give their pack a thrill.

Autumn at the Lake

the osprey perches
next to its large nest
built on the apex
of a decapitated fir

offspring fledged
and gone
mate
off fishing

scent of
surrounding guano
the only memory
of spring brood

she keens a shrill
cheereek/cheereek
over and over
and over

Bear Talk

In the winter of 1898 and 1899, 20,000 ambitious men ventured
over Chilcoot Pass into the Yukon territory as a result of an
article in the San Francisco Examiner which reported the
discovery of gold in the Klondike.

Before you hike
the 33-mile trail
over Chilcoot Pass
from Skagway, Alaska,
to Lake Bennet in the Yukon,
the rangers give "the talk."

They tell you about black bears
and grizzly bears and knowing
the critical differences. Black bears
have big ears; grizzlies have a hump,
and big claws.

A grumpy black bear can be discouraged
by loud noises and big gestures;
a grumpy grizzly is not
so easily put off.

Both are to be avoided
but I planned to hike alone through their turf,
so I carried bear deterrent spray
and was advised to make noise as I hiked
to let the bears know I am human.

If attacked by a black bear
and the spray fails its purpose,
a person should fight back.
If attacked by a grizzly,
fall to the ground, face first,
cover your head and neck, and play dead.

No information was given regarding
the poop in your pants while determining
whether your bear has big claws or big ears.
I sang every song I knew, off-key
and loudly.

SWIMMING WITH THE ANCIENTS

They come for dinner:
hundreds of whale sharks,
tiburones ballena,
to a small section
of the Caribbean
off the Yucatan coast.
Thirty-feet long—
big as a bus
curious, docile,
hungry for the plankton
that bloom here in summer.

Don mask, fins, snorkel,
drop into the water
among this graceful mass
of spotted giants,
enormous mouths,
dorsal fins,
silent—prehistoric.
Harmless but with
sensitive skin,
preferring not to touch
or be touched.
When one slides
right under me
not two feet away
I am startled.

Later, in the telling,
I will bring up the awe
leave out
the fear.

BRISTLECONE PINES

How they cluster
at ten thousand feet
on top of a swath
of glacial scree

How some endure
more than four millennia
at Great Basin National Park
on the eastern lip of Nevada

How their needles grow
in sparse bottle-brush patches
just enough for a bit
of photosynthesis

How the living parts
hew to the dead
gnarled together
for elemental protection

How it made me feel
to place my palm
on the hard crenelated trunk
that survived thousands of harsh winters

Older than empires
older than measurement
a life older than many
of our gods

TOM McKoy

Backpacker's Insight

Walking the John Muir Trail
along the roofline
of California

Flowing water
sounds like
voices

Gusting wind
sounds like
music

Falling rock
sounds like
galloping horses—

Best to pitch tent
elsewhere.

SPRING WALK ALONG THE SOUTH RIM

Hiking the Grand Canyon
the Kaibab trail is as wide
as an urban sidewalk
right turn onto the Tonto
and the trail narrows
as low bushes scratch
a network onto my shins.

Carrying enough water
to last two days
my legs tremble the first night.
Second night
Cremation Creek, third
Grapevine, fourth night
Cottonwood Creek
and out.

Even though it is desert
it rains every night
and part of the day.
Much higher a layer of snow
settles on ochre-lipped plateaus
and multi-story hoodoos.
The spectacle doesn't diminish
a penetrating chill.

TOM MCKOY

Some cacti show
fresh blossoms,
the inside
of a bright pink one
so extravagant
I lower myself carefully
to its delicate scent.

Step by step
layer upon layer
miniature and monumental
traversing the folded skirts
of time.

BIG STORM AT THE TAHOE CABIN

Sonofabitch
did it snow
that last winter
in the mountains.

Out the kitchen window
the Willys pickup truck appeared
as a gentle bump under an otherwise smooth blanket.
The Subaru disappeared completely.

The phone line still worked
and six cords of wood
kept the stove cranked
until electricity returned.

When we dug down
to reach the goats in their shed,
their bleating was no more disagreeable
than usual.

At a nearby resort
an avalanche took seven lives in an instant
and pushed through a wall to trap a young woman
under some tilted-over lockers.

Five days later
she was found alive—
all the neighbors
sobbed with relief.

At the homestead
long sessions of shoveling were sustained
by infusions of black tea
and whiskey.

When the Cat D-9 plow reached
our end-of-the-road cabin,
the driver opened the window
from his elevated perch
to give a weary wave of salvation.

ONE WINTER DAY, SLATE CREEK CANYON, CRESTED BUTTE, COLORADO

Drive to where the road ends
carry the skis up the berm

click in to the bindings
grasp the poles

start up the canyon trail
wind drives tiny ice crystals

onto my right cheek
the rhythm takes time

skis snick-snicking along
push with the left

glide with the right
plant one pole then the other

a few strides of grace
and then a stumble

back to the stride
following tracks already made

TOM McKOY

after a kilometer or two
the rhythm evens out

horsetails of powder
blow down from the ridgetop

at times the ski trail disappears
under the morning's dusting

across the creek an avalanche
has roiled a slope into huge white blocks

tracks of some small animal
vanish into a drift

the valley narrows gradually
coming to a summer cabin

a slide off the roof
covers the windows

then the wind whips me
home

Snowboarding the Big Storm

in Memory of Shawnte Willis, 1985–2010

Alpine Meadows, December 28, 2010.
Dumped fresh powder last night and still coming down,
no work; a whole day to ride.

I know this mountain; all the runs—
some so steep my body breaks the bonds of gravity,
shredding 'til my lungs burst.

Pretty windy at the summit; blinding snow
driven horizontal, but lower it's a wonderland,
the powder waist-high in the troughs;

A few completely stoked runs
with my boyfriend and the crew,
whumping through drifts up past my ears.

We huddle on the lift up,
decide to hit the backside. When we
reach the top, it is untracked heaven.

They go left, I go right.
I love it when we meet
in the middle of the hill.

Suddenly, the wind and snowfall
are too intense; the whole world has turned
to hard blowing pellets.

Cannot see a thing;
freezing snow gathers on my cheeks,
gotta bend over to stay upright.

My board stalls
in a wind-whisked tree well;
too hard to move right now.

I lean over to kick out of the binding;
sit down next to the board, tuck my nose
into my jacket, fold my arms across my chest,

Lie back, nestle into my own shape,
shut my eyes and wait—so very close
to paradise.

III

Perfect Calling

AFTERLIFE

Every day
I drive over unmarked graves;
tuft of hair, smear of blood
that once was raccoon,
deer, opossum, fox,
coyote, hawk, pigeon.
An ever-changing menagerie
ground into the surface of the road
by unconscious traffic.
After a day or two, one cannot tell
that anything lived at all.

Only the skunk gets its own special
afterlife.

A Small Sense of Catastrophe

I don't sleep so well lately.
Before dawn last Monday
a black-capped chickadee
flew through our open kitchen window.

Ellen thought it was attracted to the light
so she flipped off the switch.
I trapped its shuddering body
in a tea towel and let it out
the back door. It flew directly
at the neighbor's lighted window,
hurling itself over and over
at the unyielding pane.

TOM MCKOY

Highway Job

Every weekday morning above Highway 17
a white-breasted hawk
perched on a telephone wire
at the 1,800-foot summit
watches over a river of vehicles
flowing under his talons.

The flow proceeds
through boom and bust,
war and peace,
depression and euphoria.

He watches the morning transport
all manner of persons:
confident millionaires in starched
white shirts,
distaff attorneys with enormous
caseloads,
sheetrock workers with hangovers
as big as trucks,
coffee-stained engineers anxious about
performance appraisals.

The hawk is unimpressed by credentials
or the state of the nation.
Unencumbered by emotion
or sentiment, he is on the job
as a field mouse
strays into the open—
a few flaps, a steady glide,
whack 'em and eat 'em,
the perfect calling.

Tradeoff

Last summer a mockingbird
would wake us in the morning.
Standing on the neighbor's roof
it would reliably tweetle in the dawn.

In the fall
new neighbors came
with a cat named Chewy.
Last week I heard a thump
on the back porch.
I opened the door to see
a small swirl of gray down
and Chewy retreating homeward
with something
in his mouth.

I might complain
except
our severe gopher problem
has vanished.
The neighbor says
Chewy consumes each gopher completely.

The mockingbird has moved on.

Tom McKoy

Summer Devotion

for Ellen, whose knees are sometimes
caked in mud

When our garden
cranks out certain vegetables
my wife becomes
an Amish dervish.

Cucumbers go into
salads, soups, pickles,
and sandwiches. Zucchini
into bread, casseroles,
steamer, and barbecue.
Green beans into stews,
stir-fry, and freezer.

But it is the tomatoes
that get my attention.
For about six weeks
we are awash
in a sea of tomatoes:

Juliette, Lemon Drop, Ox-heart,
Mucha Miel, Carnella, Costa
Luto Genovese; the palette runs
from yellow through shades of red to purple.

In the second coming,
God may return
as a tomato.

A bite of last-night's Scabitha yields
a slurp of bright flavors,
sweet as well as slightly acidic.

Imperfect Domestic

Since I am a terrible cook
but anxious to demonstrate
participation and competence
in daily chores,
I often wash the dishes
after dinner.

I clear the plates from the table,
carry them to the kitchen,
stack pots, pans, bowls
next to the sink, and begin

pouring dishwashing liquid
into the deepest bowl,
fill it with hot water,
and bend to the task.

It takes me a long time,
and I use lots of hot water.
By the time I am finished,
I have conveyed both suffering
and nobility of purpose.

The next morning,
while putting dishes away,
I notice the baking dish retains
a small but distinctly discolored
greasy spot in each of its four corners.

TOM MCKOY

Bird Watching

for Tom Leskiw

Standing by the pond
binoculars in hand
she watches
to add to a life list.
The list has more than
a hundred birds:
scaly-breasted munia,
ruby-throated hummingbird,
eastern kingbird,
white-winged dove,
yellow-green vireo,
sandhill crane, and once
a red-footed booby.

Now in a low bush
she has spotted
an orange-crowned warbler.
Just as she is establishing
a positive ID, the bird
is replaced by a puff
of yellow feathers.
A peregrine falcon IDed it first.

Wake-Up Calls

five thirty a.m.
street sweeper
rumbles past the house

sleepus interruptus

cue then
the exuberant
mockingbird

Tom McKoy

IV

Remove the Marrow

CONUNDRUM

The problem with poems
is where to keep them:

scribbled in a notebook,

arranged neatly in a binder,

heaped in piles on the floor,

tossed into a shoebox,

tied with a bow in a scented drawer?

Haiku, of course,
may be kept
in a teacup.

CURRENT EVENTS

Head bent to making Sunday dinner
when a light bulb overhead
shatters inexplicably—
the meal suddenly seasoned
with tiny slivers
of frosted glass.

Only the cry of the red-tailed hawk
from the blue blue sky
or the comfort of my lover's cheek
distracts from the faint but pervasive scent
of sulfur in the air.

TOM MCKOY

Gleanings from a Lecture on Evolution

Our African ancestor, *Homo habilis*,
had no weapons—
scavenged his food from leftover kills
of lions, leopards, alpha predators.
He would scrape the flesh
with a chunk of rock,
crack the bones
with another chunk,
remove the marrow, eat,
and run,
before there was a word
for tool,
before there was a word
for fear.

RISKY BUSINESS AT THE BANK

The woman in line
in front of me
reaches the teller.
She had a difficult experience
at another branch
and needs to talk to someone.
Her legs hurt
and she carries a heavy bag.
Her son could help
but he moved to Seattle.
The woman had a savings account
but had to close it.
She would open another
but it might get hacked
by thieves, or terrorists,
or the "Occupy Movement,"
or the Republican Party.
It is such a risk.

TOM MCKOY

FRIDAY AFTERNOON ARRANGEMENT

Friday afternoon cup of joe
finds me gazing out the window
of Fin's Coffee shop
on Ocean Street in Santa Cruz.

A young man sits
in his truck in the parking lot.
He has
an arrangement.

A woman pulls into a parallel spot
with one empty space between.
A little blonde girl, maybe eight,
sits in the back seat.

The woman and the child
exit the car; the woman holds a backpack,
which she hands to the child
with a kiss on the head.

The backpack is huge on the little girl
as she walks across the space
toward the truck and the man,
who bends to give a one-armed hug.

Both watch the little girl climb into the truck.
The man turns back to face the woman,
who crosses her arms and begins to speak.

Seasonal Incidents

During a sudden
autumn snowstorm
sheep huddle
together for warmth.
They do not move.
The snow piles
higher and higher—
still
they do not move
until finally
they suffocate.

After the long winter,
after coyotes
and vultures
have fought
over scraps,
only bleached bones
and bits of wool
remain

until a new flock,
fresh with lambs,
is herded
into now green
pastures.

Tom McKoy

A Primitive Sense

Walk around a city, any city,
and watch for ginkgo trees,
unchanged for 200 million years.

A popular foliage, the bright green
fan-shaped leaves turn a fine yellow
in autumn. Originally from China
they withstand well the stress of urban life.
The females drop a fruit
which splits, rots, and smells like vomit.
Some cities plant just males, only to learn
over time some males morph to female.

Ginkgos extended along City Line Avenue
in Philadelphia where I walked
every adolescent school day
from Overbrook Station
to Episcopal Academy—
briefcase bulging
with half-completed,
chicken-scratched homework,
daydreams, and dread.

Half a century later
when I notice ginkgo fruit
on the curb by the town clock
in Santa Cruz I am careful
not to step back in time.

Divine Journey

During a drive along the California coast
the waves pound Waddell Beach;
the surf is a churn of head-high foam,
the ocean multiple strata of slate, jade, opalescence.
Clouds bundling on the horizon
ascend to billows of cumulus which soar
into patches of brilliant azure.
Who can resist marveling?
Speeding along at sixty miles an hour
it is easy to drift from the highway.

The *Santa Cruz Sentinel* might report:
"A car bearing a man drove off Highway 1
into the ocean in the vicinity of Waddell Creek.
Identification is being withheld
pending notification of next of kin."

A few weeks later an obituary
in the Sunday paper will contain
more than one spelling error.
The ashes end up settling
in a ten-by-ten cardboard box.
Since no one can locate
the latest copy of final wishes,
the box is placed on the top shelf
of a downstairs closet, along with
old Halloween costumes
and a long-forgotten paper kite.

ENCOUNTERS ON THE CAMINO FRANCES

We pilgrims constitute a polyglot moving tribe,
strung along hundreds of miles
of boots, backpacks, and dirty socks.

The Spaniards are good hosts; they share
their country, favorite foods, restaurants, and stories.
The Canadians are up early, moving rapidly.
The Dutch have walked all the way from Holland, with a limp.
The Germans are good-natured and talk about their lives.
The Romanian women have beautiful eyes
and a litany of complaints.
Only the Americans ask, *why are you walking?*

In the church at the small town of Los Arcos
the priest incants the mass in Spanish;
some understand and some do not,
yet for the faithful there is comfort in the ritual.
The rest of us must find God
other places.

Here along the Way an angel does not
descend to convey the Annunciation,
does not speak from a burning bush
but appears at the edge of a plowed field
with a three-day beard
dressed in stained blue coveralls.
Hola peregrino, el camino está allí.
The camino is that way; he points back
to the last fork in the dirt road.
I respond, *Muchas gracias,* and turn around;
the reply is always, *¡Buen Camino!*

Not a Catholic, not a Protestant
not a Jain, not a Jew
yet at every church I say,
Soy peregrino, I am a pilgrim,
will you bless me?
and every morning—
sunrise and a clear road to walk.

TOM MCKOY

Rapid Enlightenment

I am not a devotee of any particular faith or devotional study, but unlike my sister, who is atheist, I believe in a power which connects the blessings of sun, rain, earth, and life itself. Yet I want more. I am always seeking the next blessing, whatever its form. So it is the day after concluding a two-week pilgrimage on the Camino Primitivo that I find myself stepping into an elevator with a kindly looking priest on the fifth floor of the Hospedería San Martín Pinario Seminario Mayor in Santiago de Compostela.

In my deficient Spanish I tell the priest that I am not a Catholic but I am a pilgrim, and ask him to bless me. He smiles and asks me in Spanish if I am Jewish. I reply, *No I am not Jewish*. Then he asks me if I am Muslim. I reply, *No I am not Muslim*. Then he asks me if I am something that sounds like *"hudista."* I don't understand the question but we are approaching the ground floor so I reply, *Sí soy hudista*. He blesses me and we both step out of the elevator. It is only walking down the hall into the daylight I realize I had claimed that I am Buddhist.

Sacramental Fragments from a Pilgrimage

dry socks
clean sheets
hot soup
sharp cheese, crisp apple
comfortable boots
photos of family kept in a Ziploc bag
rolling fields of winter wheat
sunny day, huge blue sky
walking solitude
working cellphone
accurate guidebook
cold beer at the end of the day
cold beer at the end of the day

In the 13th century church
at Zabaldika you get a stamp
on your *credencial,*
and you can pay a half euro
to climb the tower to strike the bell just once,
a full rich resonance over a quiet mountain valley
but, if you are lucky, the best part
is a kiss on the cheek from Sister Maria
of the order of the Sacred Heart
when she wishes you, *Buen Camino*
before you step out into the rain.

At the Buddhist *albergue* in Galicia
if a pilgrim asks to see the room
the *hospitalero* replies,
No, you may not see the room,
only tourists ask to see the room.

In the cathedral at Santiago de Compostela
it is forbidden to take movies or photos
during mass, yet when the *Botafumiero*,
the incense burner, big as a Volkswagen,
is lit and swings high through the transept,
hundreds of cellphones and cameras
are held aloft and flash, trying to catch
a glimpse of the divine.

SHARED VISION NUMBER 2

so often
people pause
to offer
all of their attention
to a stunning
sunset

an astrophysicist I met
on the west coast of Hawaii
takes a photograph
of every visible sunset

he knows the dry science
regarding refraction
of light in the atmosphere
the measure of Earth turning
its reception on the individual macula

yet he recognizes
this nightly spectacle creating
a momentary communal ceremony
as evidence
of the hand
of God

TOMBSTONES IN A GRAVEYARD ON MARTHA'S VINEYARD AT THE CORNER OF GROVE AND MAIN

Mike Wallace:
Tough but Fair

Mary Wallace:
Fairly Tough

William Styron:
And so we came forth
and once again
beheld the stars

Harold Clarkson:
A year-round resident
at last

wind-ruffled treetops
my father's ashes
fall to silent ground

Tom McKoy

Hoarding Memory

> *"The future is a bucket pulled up empty."*
> —*Kathleen Flowers*

I open a sheaf of poems
from a workshop:
Spring 2003.

Blossoms spill forth

unpublished work
of poets no longer
creating in a language
we can read.
Their tenderness
for this world
overwhelms.

The reading invokes
sweet promise,
though these poets
will never know
another spring.

Evolving Ambitions

Early on
I wanted to be
Mick Jagger—
wear my hair long,
sing, *I can't get no satisfaction,*
embarrass Ed Sullivan
with a leer.

Later, it was
Gary Snyder—
be able to recite
"Ode to the West Wind"
up on a table in a pub
while half smashed,
spend months
living in a fire tower.

Then, it was
Adrienne Rich—
be fierce, brilliant,
and honorable; write about the world
through "Diving into the Wreck";
convey always a dignified literacy
and moral certitude
in poetry and prose.

Now, I want to be
a Labrador retriever—
gold-colored
would be nice.
Have a person pick up
after me; carry it for blocks
in a small plastic bag,
both of us smiling
with smug satisfaction.

Tom McKoy

GOD IN A BOX

Jesus is in a wooden crate
in the parking lot
of the Catholic Shrine
of Saint Joseph.

There is no indication
as to whether he is
coming
or going.

He is a little over five feet,
all white marble or plaster,
left hand under his robe
the other raised as if
blessing the Shrine coffee shop.

Inside the crate
a small label says,
*Customer must inspect product
within 48 hours.*

Since he has been
in the parking lot
for a number of weeks
I wonder . . .

has the church
accepted Jesus
or rejected him
due to some flaw?

In Pursuit of the Muse

The large brown dog,
muzzle going white,
gallops up the beach
on stiff legs
towards a flock
of twenty-six seagulls
resting in shallow water.
They lift lazily,
cruise overhead
and out beyond
the surf line.
The dog will never
grab a gull—
still his tail
wags wildly.

Tom McKoy

After the Poetry Reading

for Gerald Stern

For a few days
a sort of alchemy took place.
The red wine tasted richer and more complex.
A street person in his five filthy shirts
cupping a hand-rolled Bugler was suddenly
embraceable. The road-side poppies
were more brilliant red and orange.
A wave breaking off Natural Bridges
revealed an absurd luminescence.
Two doves on a telephone wire
turned their heads toward me in unison.
I laughed easily, even as I noticed
my shadow
grows shorter.

Waiting for the New Sofa

There it sits, largest object
in the room,
well past its prime;
a few cracker crumbs
from last month
wedged in the folds
of that unremarkable
hounds-tooth fabric;
a large coffee spluge
on the arm
where your cousin
gestured broadly
while conveying a point
about a political issue;
a milk stain left
by an active grandchild;
the drool on the cushion
from that long-ago night
you argued with your wife;
the slump at one end
where your distressed
female friend sat too heavily,
perspiration on her upper lip—
you offered iced tea.

The spiffy new sofa will never
see the like.

Inexplicable

All the oceans of the world
join together on my front porch.

Dolphins spin up the street
leaping and diving.

No one stops
to explain the behavior.

If my granddaughter asks,
Poppy, why do they do that?

I will have no answer.

Continuum

Spring mornings
the air on the front porch
fills with birdsong.

As dawn blooms
the singers hide in the wings.

If stage directions
instruct the lead actor
to suffer a massive heart attack
and collapse to the sidewalk

the air will still
be filled
with birdsong.

Tom McKoy

Acknowledgements

Great appreciation is due to my poetry colleagues and mentors, including Claire Braz Valentine, Ekua Omosope, Stan Rushworth, Tom Marshall, Jory Post, Tilly Washburn Shaw, Len Anderson, and the Emerald Street Poetry group (whose insight often improved the work immeasurably): Marcia Adams, Dane Cervine, Andrew Fague, Robin Lysne, Joanna Martin, Adela Najarro, Maggie Paul, Stuart Presley, Lisa Simon, Janet Trenchard, and Phil Wagner.

Also great thanks to Rosie King and the sublime seaside gatherings: Shirley Ancheta, Barbara Bloom, Angelika Frebert, Diana Hartog, Robin MacAngus, Paul Berner, Debra Spencer, Joan Safajek, and David Sullivan.

Thanks to Linda Reddy, whose article helped with organization. Thanks to Consuelo España for the Spanish translation of "Heart."Most especially thanks to my friend and sensei Joe Stroud, whose dedication to the craft of poetry serves as inspiration. Special thanks to Joan Zimmerman and Ken Weisner, who reviewed drafts of the manuscript, thereby improving pieces which were in need and casting off others which should not see the light of day.

Thanks to Jim Lamarche and Susan Cook for permission to use the painting of my old friend Gary Milburn. Thanks to my wife, Ellen McCarthy, who listens and responds with her head and heart. Thanks to my sons, Tommy, Ian and Zeph. Thanks to my sister, Linda McKoy, whose example always sets the bar high.

The following pieces previously appeared in the *Porter Gulch Review*: "Birthright," "Sacramental Fragments from a Pilgrimage," "Wounded Tea," "Waiting for the New Sofa," "Snowboarding the Big Storm."

The following pieces appeared in the online magazine *Phren-Z*: "Dream Work," "Gleanings from a Lecture on Evolution," "Bristlecone Pines," "Risky Business at the Bank," "We Go Back."

The following pieces appeared in *Unearthed, Poems by Emerald Street Poets:* "Afterlife," "Bear Talk," "In Pursuit of the Muse," "Summer Devotion."